Minds on the Fringe

Unmasking the Dark Mystique of Psychopathy and Antisocial Behavior

Freudian Trips

Copyright Page

By reading this book, the reader acknowledges and agrees that they are solely responsible for how they interpret and apply the information contained herein.

This book may also include references to other works, studies, and sources. These references are provided for further reading and exploration and do not imply endorsement or validation of the specific theories, viewpoints, or interpretations presented in those works.

Chapter I: Unmasking the Shadows

Welcome to "Minds on the Fringe: Unmasking the Dark Mystique of Psychopathy and Antisocial Behavior." This journey will take us deep into the minds of individuals who experience the world in a unique and often misunderstood way. Before we embark on this exploration, let's lay down some foundational stones to guide our path.

A. What Are We Talking About?

When we say "psychopathy," we're talking about a personality disorder that is characterized by a lack of empathy, shallow emotions, and often manipulative or antisocial behavior. In simple terms, people with psychopathy have trouble forming genuine emotional connections with others and may use manipulation or deceit to get what they want.

On the other hand, "antisocial behavior" is a term used to describe actions that harm or lack consideration for the well-being of others. This includes behaviors like lying, stealing, and displaying a general disregard for social rules and norms. While there is some overlap between psychopathy and antisocial behavior, they are not the same thing. We will delve into these differences and connections in later chapters.

B. Why Should We Care?

Understanding psychopathy and antisocial behavior is important for several reasons. For one, it can help us better navigate our interactions and relationships with those who exhibit these traits. It can also provide insight into the workings of the criminal justice system, as individuals with psychopathy or antisocial behavior are more likely to engage in criminal activity.

But most importantly, by shedding light on these conditions, we can foster empathy and compassion for those who struggle with them. After all, people with psychopathy or antisocial behavior often experience significant challenges in their personal and professional lives, and they deserve our understanding and support.

C. What's In Store?

In this book, we will explore the intricacies of psychopathy and antisocial behavior from various angles. We'll look at the historical perspective, delve into the psychology and neurobiology of these conditions, and examine their impact on society. We'll also discuss how they are assessed and diagnosed, and explore the different treatment and management options available. Along the way, we'll meet individuals who live with psychopathy or antisocial behavior and hear their stories. So, buckle up and get ready for an eye-opening journey into the minds on the fringe.

Chapter II: Tracing the Shadows: A Walk Through History

Let's turn back the pages of time and explore how our understanding of psychopathy and antisocial behavior has evolved over the years. This journey through history will shed light on how these conditions were first observed, how they came to be recognized as formal diagnoses, and some of the key figures who have shaped our understanding of them.

A. In the Beginning: Early Observations and Descriptions

Long before the terms "psychopathy" and "antisocial behavior" were coined, people observed and recorded instances of individuals exhibiting what we now recognize as traits of these conditions. Ancient civilizations like the Greeks and Romans documented cases of individuals displaying a lack of empathy, manipulative behavior, and a disregard for social norms. But it wasn't until the 19th century that these observations started to be formally documented and studied by medical professionals.

B. Putting a Name to the Shadows: Development of the Diagnoses

Fast forward to the early 20th century, when the term "psychopathy" was first introduced by German psychiatrist Emil Kraepelin. He used the term to describe individuals who exhibited antisocial behavior, emotional detachment, and a lack of moral sense. Over the years, the definition of psychopathy has evolved and expanded, with researchers and clinicians identifying key traits and behaviors associated with the condition.

Similarly, the diagnosis of antisocial personality disorder (ASPD) was developed to describe individuals who display a pervasive pattern of disregard for the rights of others, often engaging in criminal behavior and failing to conform to social norms. Today, ASPD is recognized as a formal diagnosis in the Diagnostic and Statistical Manual of Mental Disorders (DSM-5), which is a widely used diagnostic tool in the field of psychology.

C. Shadows in the Limelight: Notable Cases and Figures

Throughout history, there have been several high-profile cases and individuals that have brought attention to psychopathy and antisocial behavior. Perhaps one of the most famous cases is that of Ted Bundy, a charismatic and seemingly normal individual who was convicted of multiple brutal murders in the 1970s. Bundy's case highlighted the chilling disconnect between appearance and reality that can be seen in individuals with psychopathy.

In addition to Bundy, there have been many other cases that have captured the public's imagination and helped shape our understanding of these conditions. From notorious gangsters like Al Capone to fictional characters like Hannibal Lecter, the concept of psychopathy and antisocial behavior has permeated our culture and left an indelible mark on our collective psyche.

In conclusion, the journey through history has revealed a fascinating and sometimes chilling evolution of our understanding of psychopathy and antisocial behavior. From ancient observations to modern diagnoses, these conditions have been a source of fascination, fear, and intrigue for centuries. And as we continue to delve deeper into the mysteries of the human mind, there's no telling what new insights and discoveries await us in the shadows.

Chapter III: Peering Into the Abyss: The Psychopathic Mind

As we delve into the fascinating and often perplexing world of psychopathy, it's essential to understand what's happening in the minds of individuals with this condition. In this chapter, we'll explore the brain structure and function, emotional processing, and key personality traits that define psychopathy.

A. The Brain's Inner Workings

When we peek inside the brain of someone with psychopathy, we notice some distinct differences. Studies have shown that certain areas of the brain, particularly those responsible for emotions and impulse control, may not function the same way as they do in the general population. These differences might explain why individuals with psychopathy often struggle with forming emotional connections and exhibit impulsive behavior.

B. Emotional Processing and Empathy

One of the hallmarks of psychopathy is a lack of empathy, which is the ability to understand and share the feelings of others. This doesn't necessarily mean that individuals with psychopathy are completely devoid of emotions; instead, they may experience emotions in a shallow or fleeting way. This diminished emotional experience can make it challenging for them to connect with others on a deeper, more meaningful level.

C. Personality Traits and Characteristics

When we talk about the personality of someone with psychopathy, several key traits stand out. These individuals often exhibit a charming and charismatic facade, which can be deceiving and mask their true intentions. They might also engage in manipulative and deceitful behavior, taking advantage of others to achieve their goals. Other common traits include a grandiose sense of self, a lack of remorse or guilt, and a propensity for boredom and seeking out new and exciting experiences, often at the expense of others.

In conclusion, the psychopathic mind is a complex and often misunderstood landscape. While the lack of empathy and manipulative behavior can make individuals with psychopathy seem cold and unfeeling, it's essential to remember that these traits are often rooted in differences in brain structure and function. By continuing to explore and understand these differences, we can gain valuable insights into the nature of psychopathy and develop more effective interventions and support for those affected by this condition.

Chapter IV: Stepping Over the Line: Understanding Antisocial Behavior

As we continue our exploration of the dark and mysterious world of psychopathy, let's turn our attention to antisocial behavior, a related but distinct concept that often gets confused with psychopathy. In this chapter, we will clarify what antisocial behavior is, how it relates to psychopathy, and what factors may contribute to its development.

A. Drawing the Line: Definition and Diagnostic Criteria

Antisocial behavior refers to actions that harm or lack consideration for the well-being of others. This includes a range of behaviors, such as lying, stealing, and generally disregarding social rules and norms. In more severe cases, antisocial behavior may be classified as Antisocial Personality Disorder (ASPD), which is a recognized mental health condition. To be diagnosed with ASPD, an individual must meet specific criteria outlined in the Diagnostic and Statistical Manual of Mental Disorders (DSM-5), such as a pattern of disregarding the rights of others, failing to conform to social norms, and displaying a lack of remorse for their actions.

B. The Intersecting Paths: Relationship with Psychopathy

While antisocial behavior and psychopathy share some similarities, they are not the same thing. All individuals with psychopathy display antisocial behavior, but not all individuals with antisocial behavior have psychopathy. The key difference lies in the emotional component – individuals with psychopathy have a notable lack of empathy and emotional connection, whereas those with antisocial behavior may still be capable of forming emotional bonds and experiencing empathy, albeit in a diminished capacity.

C. Peeling Back the Layers: Causes and Risk Factors

Several factors may contribute to the development of antisocial behavior, ranging from genetics and brain structure to environmental influences. Some individuals may have a genetic predisposition to antisocial behavior, with research suggesting that certain genes may play a role in regulating emotions and impulse control. Brain abnormalities, particularly in areas responsible for emotions and decision-making, may also contribute to antisocial behavior. Additionally, environmental factors such as childhood trauma, exposure to violence, and inconsistent parenting can play a significant role in shaping an individual's behavior and personality.

In conclusion, antisocial behavior is a complex and multifaceted phenomenon that can be influenced by a range of genetic, neurological, and environmental factors. By exploring the intricacies of antisocial behavior and its relationship with psychopathy, we can gain a deeper understanding of these conditions and develop more effective interventions to support individuals affected by them.

Chapter V: Where Shadows Meet: The Intersection of Psychopathy and Antisocial Behavior

We've explored the realms of psychopathy and antisocial behavior separately, but what happens when these two worlds collide? In this chapter, we'll delve into the overlap between psychopathy and antisocial behavior, provide real-life examples to illustrate their intersection, and discuss the implications for treatment and management.

A. A Venn Diagram of Shadows: Overlapping and Distinct Features

Think of psychopathy and antisocial behavior as two circles in a Venn diagram. In the overlapping section, you'll find traits such as a disregard for social norms and a propensity for deceitful and manipulative behavior. But each circle also has its unique characteristics. For psychopathy, this includes a profound lack of empathy and emotional depth, while for antisocial behavior, it might be a tendency to engage in criminal activities or acts that harm others.

B. Stories from the Shadows: Case Studies and Examples

To bring this intersection to life, let's look at some real-world examples. Take the case of John, a charismatic individual who could easily charm those around him. Underneath this facade, however, John exhibited a clear lack of empathy and frequently manipulated others to get what he wanted. In this case, John's behavior demonstrates characteristics of both psychopathy and antisocial behavior. On the flip side, you have someone like Alex, who has a long history of criminal activity and shows a blatant disregard for the rights of others, fitting the criteria for antisocial behavior, but still capable of forming emotional bonds and experiencing empathy, thus not fitting the criteria for psychopathy.

C. Navigating the Shadows: Implications for Treatment and Management

The intersection of psychopathy and antisocial behavior has significant implications for treatment and management. Traditional therapeutic approaches that rely on building emotional connections may not be effective for individuals with psychopathy due to their lack of empathy. Instead, alternative methods that focus on changing behaviors and developing social skills may be more beneficial. For those with antisocial behavior, addressing underlying factors such as trauma or substance abuse can be crucial in mitigating harmful behaviors. Regardless of the approach, it's essential to tailor treatments to the individual's needs, taking into account the unique blend of psychopathy and antisocial traits they may exhibit.

In conclusion, while psychopathy and antisocial behavior share some common ground, they are distinct conditions with unique features. By understanding their intersection and the implications for treatment and management, we can develop more effective strategies to support individuals affected by these conditions and ultimately work towards a safer and more harmonious society.

Chapter VI: Shadows on Society: Unraveling the Ripple Effects

The intriguing and often misunderstood worlds of psychopathy and antisocial behavior are not confined to individuals; they cast their shadows far and wide, affecting society as a whole. This chapter will explore the impact on criminal activity, delve into the presence of psychopathy in professional settings, and examine how the media shapes our understanding of these complex conditions.

A. Behind Bars and Beyond: Criminal Activity and Justice System Interactions

It's not surprising that there is a significant overlap between antisocial behavior, psychopathy, and criminal activity. Individuals exhibiting these traits are more likely to engage in acts that harm others, from theft to more severe crimes. This brings them into frequent contact with the criminal justice system. However, it's important to note that not everyone with antisocial traits or psychopathy engages in criminal activities; these conditions can manifest in various ways, some more subtle than others.

B. Suits and Shadows: Psychopathy in the Corporate World and Other Professional Settings

While we often associate psychopathy with criminal behavior, it can also manifest in less obvious ways. Believe it or not, some traits associated with psychopathy, such as charm and a willingness to take risks, can be advantageous in the corporate world and other professional settings. However, this can also lead to unethical behavior, manipulation, and a disregard for the well-being of others, creating a toxic work environment.

C. Through the Looking Glass: The Media's Portrayal and Public Perception

The media plays a significant role in shaping our understanding of psychopathy and antisocial behavior. Films and television shows often depict individuals with these conditions as cold-hearted villains or charming but dangerous characters. While these portrayals can be entertaining, they also contribute to the stigma surrounding these conditions and may not accurately represent the diversity of experiences of those affected by them. It's crucial to approach these media depictions with a critical eye and seek out accurate information to form a well-rounded understanding.

In conclusion, psychopathy and antisocial behavior can profoundly impact society, from criminal activity and interactions with the justice system to their presence in professional settings and portrayal in the media. By acknowledging these impacts and striving to understand the complexities of these conditions, we can work towards a more informed and compassionate society that supports individuals affected by psychopathy and antisocial behavior while also protecting the well-being of the broader community.

Chapter VII: Unraveling the Mystery: Assessing and Diagnosing the Shadows

Understanding and identifying psychopathy and antisocial behavior can be a complex process, much like trying to solve a puzzle without having all the pieces. This chapter will guide you through the tools and methods used by professionals, highlight the challenges faced in assessment and diagnosis, and explore the exciting future directions in research.

A. The Detective's Toolkit: Tools and Methods

To assess psychopathy and antisocial behavior, professionals use a combination of interviews, questionnaires, and sometimes even brain imaging. One of the most widely used tools is the Hare Psychopathy Checklist-Revised (PCL-R), which helps assess psychopathic traits. There are also various other assessment tools and methods specifically designed to diagnose antisocial personality disorder. These assessments aim to gather as much information as possible to create a clear picture of the individual's behaviors, thoughts, and feelings.

B. Navigating the Fog: Challenges and Limitations

However, this process is not without its challenges. One significant challenge is the possibility of individuals not being truthful during assessments, as some might try to hide their antisocial traits or psychopathic tendencies. Additionally, there is ongoing debate among professionals about the definition and criteria for these conditions, which can make diagnosis even more complicated.

C. Peering into the Future: Future Directions in Research and Assessment

Despite these challenges, there are exciting developments on the horizon. Researchers are exploring new ways to understand the brain's role in psychopathy and antisocial behavior, which could lead to more accurate assessment tools. Additionally, there is an increasing focus on developing interventions and treatments specifically tailored to these conditions. As we continue to make advancements in this field, our ability to assess and support individuals affected by psychopathy and antisocial behavior will only improve.

In conclusion, assessing and diagnosing psychopathy and antisocial behavior is a multifaceted process that requires careful consideration and a comprehensive approach. By continuing to refine our tools and methods and exploring new directions in research, we can gain a deeper understanding of these conditions and develop effective strategies to support individuals affected by them.

Chapter VIII: Bringing Light to the Shadows: Treatment and Management

When we step into the world of treating and managing psychopathy and antisocial behavior, we find ourselves in a landscape filled with both hope and challenge. In this chapter, we'll explore the current approaches to treatment, evaluate their effectiveness, and delve into the controversies and ethical considerations that surround this delicate subject.

A. Finding the Right Tools: Current Approaches and Interventions

A range of treatments and management strategies are available for individuals with psychopathy and antisocial behavior, from therapy and counseling to medication in some cases. Cognitive-behavioral therapy (CBT) is a commonly used approach, focusing on changing maladaptive thought patterns and behaviors. In more severe cases, especially when the individual poses a risk to others, long-term management and monitoring may be necessary.

B. Measuring the Shadows: Effectiveness and Outcomes

The effectiveness of treatment for psychopathy and antisocial behavior is a topic of ongoing research and debate. While some individuals respond well to treatment, others may show little to no improvement. The challenge lies in the nature of these conditions, as the lack of empathy and remorse in psychopathy and the deep-seated behavioral patterns in antisocial behavior can be difficult to change.

C. Navigating the Ethical Maze: Controversies and Ethical Considerations

When it comes to treating psychopathy and antisocial behavior, ethical considerations and controversies abound. One significant debate revolves around the use of medication to manage symptoms, as some argue that this approach may be more about controlling behavior than providing meaningful treatment. Another controversy concerns the treatment of individuals who have not yet committed a crime but are identified as having psychopathic traits or antisocial tendencies. Balancing the need to protect society while respecting the individual's rights and autonomy is a complex and often contentious issue.

In conclusion, the journey towards effective treatment and management of psychopathy and antisocial behavior is filled with twists and turns. While we have made significant strides in developing interventions and strategies to support individuals affected by these conditions, much work remains to be done. By continuing to explore new approaches, rigorously evaluate the effectiveness of existing treatments, and carefully consider the ethical implications, we can shed light on the shadows that surround psychopathy and antisocial behavior and work towards a brighter, more hopeful future.

Chapter IX: Seeds of Change: Prevention and the Road Ahead

In our journey through the dark forest of psychopathy and antisocial behavior, we now find ourselves at a crossroads, looking towards the future. In this chapter, we will explore the promising avenues of prevention, delve into the intricate web of public policy and legal implications, and peer into the horizon of ongoing research.

A. Planting the Seeds: Early Identification and Intervention

When it comes to preventing the full-blown manifestation of psychopathy and antisocial behavior, early identification and intervention are key. Just like catching a weed before it takes over a garden, recognizing the early signs and providing appropriate support can make all the difference. This could involve therapy, educational support, or other interventions designed to foster empathy, emotional regulation, and positive social behaviors.

B. Shaping the Landscape: Public Policy and Legal Implications

The realm of public policy and law plays a crucial role in managing and preventing antisocial behavior and psychopathy. Laws and regulations can provide a framework for identifying, treating, and in some cases, containing individuals who exhibit these behaviors. However, this opens up a Pandora's box of ethical and legal dilemmas, such as the balance between protecting society and respecting individual rights. Navigating this intricate landscape requires ongoing dialogue and collaboration between policymakers, legal experts, and mental health professionals.

C. Charting the Unexplored: Ongoing Research and Unanswered Questions

While we have come a long way in our understanding of psychopathy and antisocial behavior, the horizon is still filled with unanswered questions and uncharted territories. Ongoing research is crucial to unraveling the mysteries of these conditions, from the underlying biological and environmental factors to the development of effective treatments and preventive strategies. Only by continuing to ask questions and seek answers can we hope to find the light at the end of the tunnel.

In conclusion, the path towards a brighter future in preventing and managing psychopathy and antisocial behavior is a challenging yet hopeful one. By focusing on early identification and intervention, navigating the complexities of public policy and law, and committing to ongoing research, we can pave the way for a society that is both compassionate and protected from the shadows of these perplexing conditions.

Emerging from the Shadows: A Final Reflection

As we stand at the crossroads of our journey through the world of psychopathy and antisocial behavior, let's take a moment to reflect on the key points we've explored together.

A. Illuminating the Path: Summary of Key Points

We began by defining psychopathy and antisocial behavior, shedding light on the importance of understanding these complex conditions. We then traveled back in time to witness the evolution of these diagnoses and meet some of the notable figures who have shaped our understanding of them.

Next, we delved into the inner workings of the psychopathic mind, unraveling the mysteries of brain structure, emotional processing, and personality traits. Our journey then took us to the realm of antisocial behavior, where we explored the defining characteristics, its relationship with psychopathy, and the various factors that contribute to its development.

The intersection of psychopathy and antisocial behavior was our next stop, where we examined their overlapping and distinct features, and gained insights through real-life examples and case studies.

From there, we ventured into the societal impacts of these conditions, exploring their effects on criminal activity, professional settings, and media portrayals. The intricate world of assessment and diagnosis was our next destination, where we learned about the tools and challenges that professionals face in identifying these conditions.

Treatment and management strategies were our next focus, where we examined the current approaches, their effectiveness, and the ethical dilemmas that arise. Our journey then led us to the promising land of prevention and the future, where we discussed the importance of early intervention, public policy, and ongoing research.

In conclusion, while the shadows of psychopathy and antisocial behavior may seem daunting, our exploration has armed us with knowledge and understanding. By continuing to shed light on these conditions, we can work towards a future where individuals affected by them receive the support they need, and society is protected from their potential harms. So, let's step forward with hope and determination, knowing that knowledge is the first step towards positive change.

About Freudian Trips

Welcome to Freudian Trips, your dedicated platform for diving deep into the world of psychology. We are more than just a YouTube channel or a book publisher. We are a beacon of enlightenment, making complex psychological concepts accessible and engaging for all.

Our YouTube channel is a rich repository of psychology made simple. We take the profound and often complex ideas from the world of psychology and break them down into digestible, easy-to-understand content. From the foundational theories of Freud to the cognitive insights of Piaget, we cover a broad spectrum of psychological schools and thoughts, making psychology accessible to everyone, regardless of their background or prior knowledge.

As a book publisher, we take the same approach, transforming intricate psychological theories into comprehensible narratives. Our books are not just collections of words, but vessels of wisdom that make psychology approachable and relatable. We believe that psychology should not be confined to academic circles, but should be available to all who seek to understand the human mind and behavior.

At Freudian Trips, we believe in the power of curiosity and the pursuit of knowledge. We are here to stoke the fires of your curiosity, to guide you on your intellectual journey, and to help you navigate the fascinating world of psychology.

If you are someone who is not afraid to question, to explore, and to learn, then you are in the right place. Join us on this journey of exploration, as we make psychology easy to understand, one concept at a time.

Be sure to visit our Youtube channel at: www.freudiantrips.com/youtube

You can also visit us on the web at www.freudiantrips.com

Welcome to The Freudian Trip community. Stay curious. Stay enlightened.